Acknowledgments:
The limerick on page 29 by Gelett Burgess appears by permission of Dover Publications Inc., New York, and the limericks on pages 4 and 20 are by Joan Roy. The two puzzles on page 55 are by Richard Siddons.

First Edition

The LADYBIRD book of
JOKES RIDDLES and RHYMES

compiled by Joyce and Peter Young

with illustrations by

Martin Aitchison   Bobbie Craig
Rosemary Farrell   James Hodgson
Frank Humphris   Keith Logan
Brian Price Thomas

The elephant's a pretty bird,
It hops from bough to bough.
It makes its nest in the rhubarb tree
And whistles like a cow.

'Have you ever seen a man-eating lion, Potterton?'
'No, but I have seen a man eating chicken.'

What is the difference
between a flea and an elephant?
*An elephant can have fleas
but a flea can't have elephants!*

Have Fun

**Find the way
to the top of
the mountain.**

2

There was a young man of Bengal
Who went to a fancy-dress ball.
  He thought he would risk it
  And dressed as a biscuit
But a dog ate him up in the hall.

What cup can't you drink from?
A buttercup!
What other cup can't you drink from?
A hiccup!

'Knock, knock!'
'Who's there?'
'Amos.'
'Amos who?'
'A mosquito!'

'Our dog has no nose.'
'Poor dog! How does he smell?'
'Terrible!'

Tongue Twister
Bella buys black bug's blood.

3

Tongue Twister
She sells sea-shells on the sea-shore.

'My baby sister has been walking
for four months.'
'She must be tired!'

What's the best thing to put in a pie?
Your teeth!

THE
LION
TAMER
by
CLAUDE BODDIE

'Potterton, which animal
is always laughing?'
'A happy-potamus, of course.'

There was a young man from Dundee
Who climbed a very high tree.
   He felt such a clown,
   He couldn't get down —
He's been there since 1903.

4

Have Fun

How many animals can you find?

Tongue Twister
The sun will surely shine soon.

There once was a young man called Fred
Who always slept under the bed.
   Said his friends, ''Oh, how strange!
   It's time for a change.''
So he sleeps 'neath the bookcase instead.

It's done under the mistletoe,
It's done under the rose.
But the proper place to kiss,
                you know,
Is just under the nose.

'Do you know the story
of the bed?'
'No. What is it?'
'I've not made it up yet!'

'I'm writing a letter to my sister.'
'Don't be silly, Willie,
you can't write.'
'It doesn't matter –
she can't read!'

A Trick to Amaze Your Friends!
Show your friends a sieve and tell them
you can carry water in it.
They won't believe you. Then put
some ice-cubes in the sieve!

There was an Old Man with a beard
Who said, 'It is just as I feared! –
    Four Larks and a Wren,
    Two Owls and a Hen,
Have all built their nests in my beard!'
Edward Lear

6

'Potterton, what does minimum mean?'
'A little mother.'

'Doctor, doctor! I can't sleep!'
'Try lying on the edge of the bed.
You'll soon drop off!'

THE CANNIBAL CHIEF

BY HENRIETTA MAN

Have Fun

**Trace the tangled lines
to find which cat
has caught which fish.**

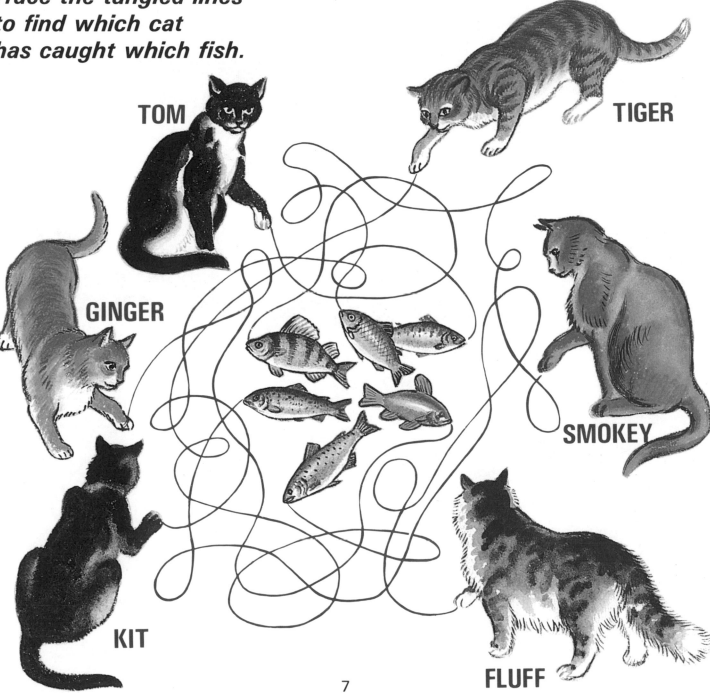

TOM

TIGER

GINGER

SMOKEY

KIT

FLUFF

A diner, while dining at Crewe,
Found a rather large mouse in his stew.
    Said the waiter, 'Don't shout
    Or wave it about –
Or the rest will be wanting one too!'

Tongue Twister
A noisy noise annoys an oyster.

'My Dad can play the piano by ear.'
'That's nothing! My Dad fiddles
with his whiskers!'

Where do tadpoles change
into frogs?
In the croakroom!

'Knock, knock!'
'Who's there?'
'Mars.'
'Mars who?'
'Marzipan!'

'Potterton, what do you get
if you cross a hippopotamus
with a kangaroo?'
'A hoppy-potamus.'

The Snapping Snort-hopper
From which animals did
the Snapping Snort-hopper
get all his parts?

Why should you never shave
a man with an umbrella?
It's better to use a razor!

I wish I were a little grub
With whiskers on my tummy.
I'd climb into a honey pot
And make my tummy gummy.

9

'Where does your mother
come from?'
'Alaska.'
'Don't bother,
I'll ask her myself!'

Howler
A barbecue
is a lot of people
waiting to get their hair cut

What's worse than a giraffe
with a sore throat?
A centipede with chilblains!

'Postman, have you any letters for Mike Howe?'
'No, sir. No letters for your cow — or your horse either!'

'Have you heard the story
about the dust-bin?'
'No, what is it?'
'It's just a load of rubbish!'

Tongue Twister
The shop that sells short socks, shuts soon.

Have Fun

**Find the names of two girls
and two boys
hidden in the square.
You can move from one
letter to a neighbouring
letter, in any direction.
Each letter is used
only once.**

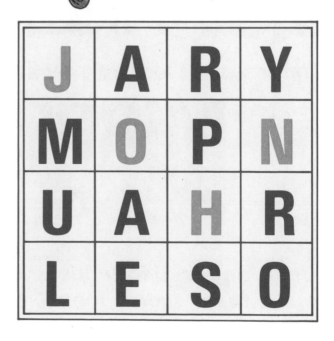

J	A	R	Y
M	O	P	N
U	A	H	R
L	E	S	O

Lady May I try on that dress in the window?
Assistant Certainly, madam,
but I think it would be better
if you tried it on in the changing room!

The sausage is a cunning bird
With feathers bright and wavy,
It skates around the frying pan —
And makes its nest in gravy.

What did the biscuits say to the peanuts?
You're nuts and we're crackers!

Have Fun

These words look like what they mean.

MIRROR

Now, on a separate piece of paper,
make these words look like what they mean —
SHIVER   RAINBOW   JUMPING

Why do bees hum?
Because they've forgotten the words!

Tongue Twister
A cup of coffee in a copper coffee pot.

There was a young fellow named Max
Who filled all his pockets with tacks.
   He thought he was clever
   Although he could never
Sit down in a chair and relax.

Why did the dog wear brown boots?
Because his black ones were being mended!

'Waiter, how long will my sausages be?'

'About three or four inches, sir.'

'*What's in between the North Pole
and the South Pole, Potterton?*'
'*Telegraph wires, of course.*'

An old polar bear in the zoo
Could always find something to do.
   It bored him, you know,
   To walk to and fro –
So he turned round and walked fro and to.

Dogs delight to bark and bite
And little birds to sing.
And if you sit on a red hot brick
It's a sign of an early spring.

THE BIG BLAST BY DINAH MITE

What would happen if pigs could fly?
Bacon would go up!

'Darling, your ears are like petals.'
'Rose petals, darling?'
'No – bicycle pedals!'

Find the dog's name hidden in his picture!

'Waiter, have you got frogs' legs?'
'Yes, sir.'
'Then hop into the kitchen and fetch me a steak!'

There was a young boy in the choir
Whose voice it got higher and higher.
  It reached such a height
  It went out of sight
And they found it next day on the spire.

Teacher
What is a gnome, Nellie?
Nellie
An 'ome's an 'ouse, Miss.

Who is hidden in this jumbled word?

GIMANICA

16

Tongue Twister
This thistle seems like that thistle.

'Potterton, if you put ten ducks
in a crate, what would you have?'
'A box of quackers.'

'Do you know the story
of the pat of butter?'
'No. What is it?'
'I won't tell you –
you might spread it!'

'Who's that at the door?'
'The Invisible Man.'
'Tell him I can't see him!'

I wish I were a kangaroo,
I would enjoy the hopping,
And I would have a place
                    for things
I buy when I go shopping!

J.Y

SPONGE
CAKE

ECLAIRS

17

There was a young lady of Leeds
Who swallowed a packet of seeds.
   In less than an hour
   Her nose was in flower
And her head was covered in weeds.

'Doctor, doctor, my hair's
falling out. Can you give me
something to keep it in?'
'How about this paper bag?'

What do you get if you cross
a tractor with a dog?
A land-rover!

The Old Goat
by E Butts

Howler
A myth is a lady moth.

Why is a chicken like a guitar?
They both need plucking!

What has horns and says 'Oom'?
A backward cow!

Have Fun

Find where the gold is hidden!

The secret message below is in the following code

A=Z B=Y C=X D=W E=V F=U G=T H=S I=R

J=Q K=P L=O M=N N=M O=L P=K Q=J R=I

S=H T=G U=F V=E W=D X=C Y=B Z=A

Can you read it?

RM TFOXS
ULLG LU HNLPVB XZMBLM ZG GSV
BLF DROO URMW NLFMGZRM
NRMV ZMWTL LM GROO VSRMW HGIRPV
ILXP UZOO. KLMB VCKIVHH YB
TLOW RH SRWWVM RM GSV ILLU
OFXPB HGIRPV HSZXP
VCKIVHH RM GSV ILLU

19

'Where do you come from, Potterton?'
'Africa.'
'What part?'
'All of me, of course.'

'Who's that at the door?'
'A man with a drum.'
'Tell him to beat it!'

What do you do with a sick wasp?
Take it to the wasp-ital!

There was a old man from Hong Kong
Whose name was terribly long.
   He thought he could change it,
   Perhaps re-arrange it —
But then he found out he was Wong.

Find the twins! Name the two monkeys that look alike.

Rex   **Jinx**   **Tex**   **Max**   **Bax**

An accident happened to my brother Jim,
Someone threw a tomato at him.
Tomatoes are juicy and don't hurt the skin –
This one was different. It was packed in a tin!

Willie What are you going to do
with that manure, Dad?
Father Put it on my rhubarb.
Willie Funny –
I always put custard on mine!

The other day upon the stair
I saw a man who wasn't there.
He wasn't there again today –
I wish that man would go away!

'Doctor, doctor, I snore so loudly
I keep myself awake.'
'You'd better sleep in another room.'

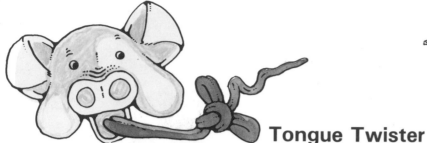

Tongue Twister
Beat him with a black-backed back brush!

How do you know that policemen
are strong?
*Because they hold up
all the traffic with one hand!*

There was a young farmer called Briggs
Who had two intelligent pigs.
  One could play 'Home Sweet Home'
  On a paper and comb,
And the other could dance Irish jigs.

Who wears the biggest hat in the world?
The man with the biggest head!

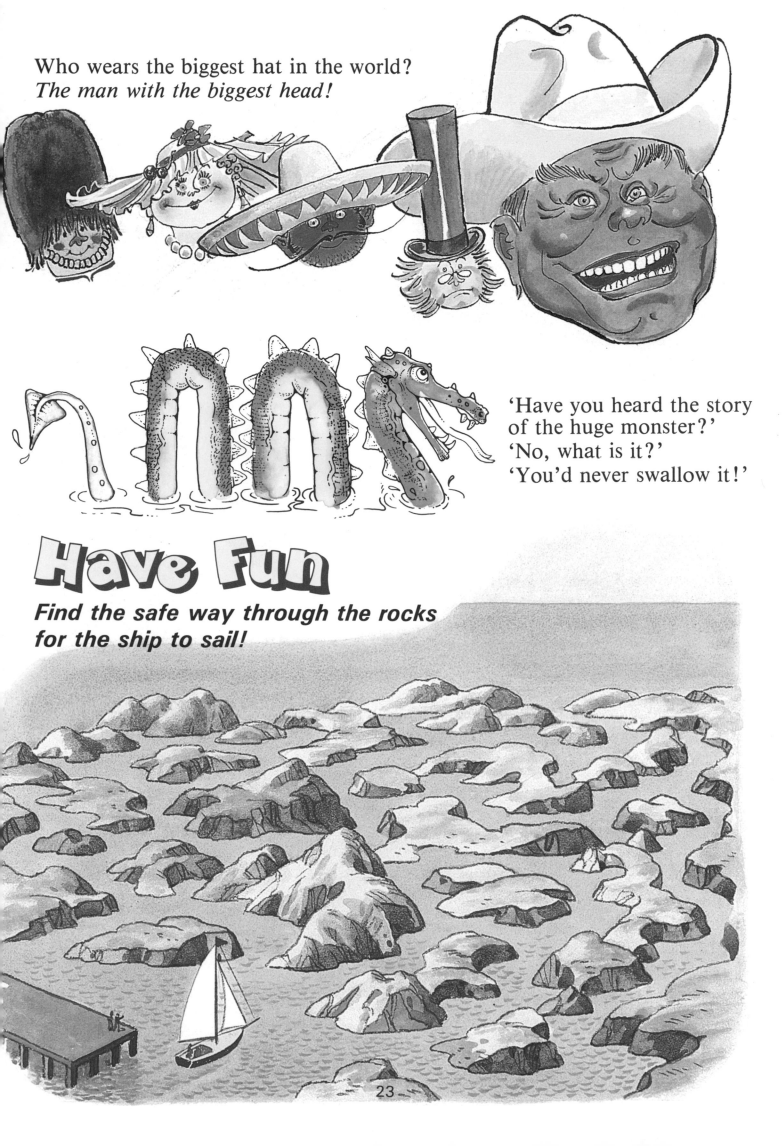

'Have you heard the story
of the huge monster?'
'No, what is it?'
'You'd never swallow it!'

Have Fun

**Find the safe way through the rocks
for the ship to sail!**

'Knock, knock!'
'Who's there?'
'Boo.'
'Boo who?'
'Don't cry – I'm only joking!'

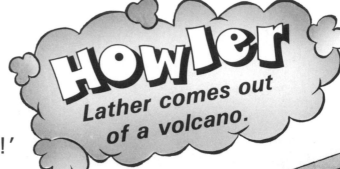

Willie, hitting at a ball,
Hit it right into the hall.
Through the door came Uncle Bill –
His two front teeth are missing still.

Have Fun

**Find the names of the five animals hidden in the square.
You can move from one letter to a neighbouring letter, in any direction.
Each letter is used only once.**

S	H	I	Z	E
N	P	C	A	B
R	A	P	R	M
E	O	K	A	E
G	I	T	E	L

'Potterton, why do some cows wear bells?'
'Oh, because their horns don't work.'

What's flat and yellow
and turns round
very slowly?
*A long-playing
pancake!*

'How many sheep
have you, Farmer Green?'
'I don't know. Every time
I start counting them,
I fall asleep.'

How did the space chicken get out of its egg?
Through the egg-scape hatch!

A
QUICK
SNACK
BY
ROLAND
BUTTER

Little Willie with his sock
Hit the cuckoo in the clock.
Father asked, 'Why won't it tick?'
Willie said, 'I think it's sick.'

'My pal and I
have been hunting.
We got four rabbits
and a potfer.'
'What's a potfer?'
'To cook the rabbits in.'

Tongue Twister
Toy boat. Toy boat.

I eat my peas with honey,
I've done so all my life.
It makes the peas taste funny —
But it keeps them on my knife!

The Richest Man in the World by Ivor Fortune

Where would you find
a pre-historic cow?
In a moo-seum!

Have Fun

**Whose present? Trace the tangled strings
to find who has which present.**

'Doctor, doctor, I keep thinking I'm the Moon!'
'I can't see you now – come back tonight.'

'Do you know the story
of the Manx cat?'
'No, what is it?'
'There's no tail to tell!'

'Knock, knock!'
'Who's there?'
'Mister.'
'Mister who?'
'Mister –
but I'll hit her next time!'

How many animals can you find?

There was a young man from Dunoon
Who always ate soup with a fork,
   For he said, 'As I eat
   Neither fish, fowl nor flesh
I should finish my dinner too quick.'

P.S. *About that 'Man from Dunoon' – should it be*

There was a young man from Dunoon
Who always ate cake with a spoon,
   For he said, 'As I eat
   Neither fish, fowl nor meat
I should finish my dinner too soon.'

or . . . . ?
There was an old man from New Yoi
Who always ate soup with a fork,
   For he said, 'As I wish
   Neither fowl, flesh nor fish
I still have the time for a walk.'

28

'Potterton, which is further away, Africa or the moon?'
'Africa, I'm sure. I can see the moon, but I can't see Africa.'

Tongue Twister
Red leather, yellow leather. Red leather, yellow leather.

The bottle of scent that Willie sent
Was most unpleasant to Millicent;
   Her thanks were so cold
    They quarrelled, I'm told,
About that silly scent Willie sent Millicent.

I wish that my room had a floor,
I don't care so much for a door,
   But this walking around
    Without touching the ground
Is getting to be quite a bore.

29

Lady Be quick, please. I want a mouse-trap.
I'm in a hurry to catch a train.
Assistant Sorry, lady. We haven't any
as big as that.

How do you start
a teddy-bear race?
Say, 'Ready, teddy, go!'

Have Fun

The Lesser Long-necked Eaglostricock

From which birds did the Eaglostricock get all his parts?

There was a young lady called Lynne
Who was so terribly thin
    That when she was made
    To drink lemonade
She slipped through the straw and fell in.

Why do policemen wear blue braces?
To hold their trousers up!

Have Fun

**Find the horse's name
hidden in his picture.**

Tongue Twister
Sixty shy soldiers.
Sixty shy soldiers.

'My car won't go.'
'Is the battery flat?'
'I don't know.
What shape should it be?'

'How would you know
if an elephant was in bed with you?'
'Look for the big E
on his pyjama pocket!'

CRISPS

E

What do you get if you cross a rabbit
with a kangaroo?
A fur coat with big pockets!

'Willie, wash your hands
before you play the piano!'
'Don't worry, Mum.
I'll only play on the black keys.'

There once were three owls in a wood
Who sang songs whenever they could.
    What the words were about
    You couldn't make out
But it seemed to be doing them good.

There was a young man of Luton
Went out with his birthday suit on.
　　His friends said, 'Oh Jack,
　　You must really go back!'
So he did – and put his boots on.

P.Y.

Howler
An octopus is eight cats joined together.

How can you stop a rooster
crowing on Monday morning?
Eat him for Sunday dinner!

'My uncle has a wooden leg!'
'That's nothing! My aunt has
a wooden chest!'

Have Fun

JORUNCOR

'Have you ever seen a cricket bat, Potterton?'
'Oh yes – and I've seen a goldfish bowl, too.'

If pig skins make good shoes, what do banana skins make? *Good slippers!*

'Do you know the story of the umbrella?'
'No, tell me about it.'
'It's over your head!'

Why did Dick Turpin take a bundle of hay to bed with him? *To feed his nightmare!*

'Who's that at the door?'
'A man with a wooden leg.'
'Tell him to hop it!'

'Why does a giraffe have a long neck, Potterton?'
'Because his head is so far from his body.'

'Knock, knock!'
'Who's there?'
'Howard.'
'Howard who?'
'Howard you like to be out in the cold?'

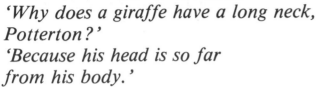

'Nellie, be quiet!
Your father's trying to read.'

'Isn't he slow –
I learned years ago!'

There once was a girl of New York
Whose body was lighter than cork.
　　She had to be fed
　　On a diet of lead
Before she went out for a walk.

When is it bad luck
to see a black cat?

When you're a mouse!

On a cold and frosty morning
Our Egbert rode his bicycle,
Did not heed his father's warning,
Now Egbert is an icicle.

P.Y.

'Does your dog like children?'
'Yes, but he prefers biscuits
and bones.'

Howler
Hailstones are hard-boiled rain.

Have Fun

Patch

Fido

Ricky

Chap

Bonzo

Skippy

Find the twins! Name the two dogs who look alike.

What has six legs, four ears and a tail?
A man on a horse.

'Have you heard the story of the Tower of London?'
'No, what is it?'
'It's not up your street!'

There was a young lady of Cork
Whose Dad kept a shop that sold pork.
    He found for his daughter
    A juggler who taught her
To balance green peas on her fork.

Have Fun

Make music with your own shaker! Put a handful of rice or dried peas in a tin and fix the lid really tight. Now you can shake and rattle as you sing or listen to your favourite music. Experiment with different amounts of different things such as sand, tiny stones, beads or beans (dried not baked!) to get a sound you really like.

What can you do for a pig
with a sore head?
Rub its head with oinkment!

'Nellie, your socks are inside out!'
'I know – but there are holes
on the other side.'

Oh, have you seen the Jub-jub bird
With toes so pink and curly?
It wears a candle in its ear
And goes to bed quite early!

J.Y.

How did the sparrow get down
from the space-ship?
By sparrow chute!

'I'm glad I wasn't born in Spain.'
'Why, Potterton?'
'I can't speak Spanish.'

'Knock, knock!'
'Who's there?'
'Cook.'
'Cook who?'
'I know you are!'

Tongue Twister
Peggy Babcock. Peggy Babcock.

39

'Is this hair tonic
any good?'
'It's marvellous, sir
Last week a custom
pulled the cork out
with his teeth.
Now he's got
a bushy moustache

'Waiter, do you serve shrimps?'
'We serve anyone, sir.
We don't mind what size you are!'

Why do people laugh up their sleeves?
That's where their funny-bones are!

Have Fun

How many everyday things can you find?

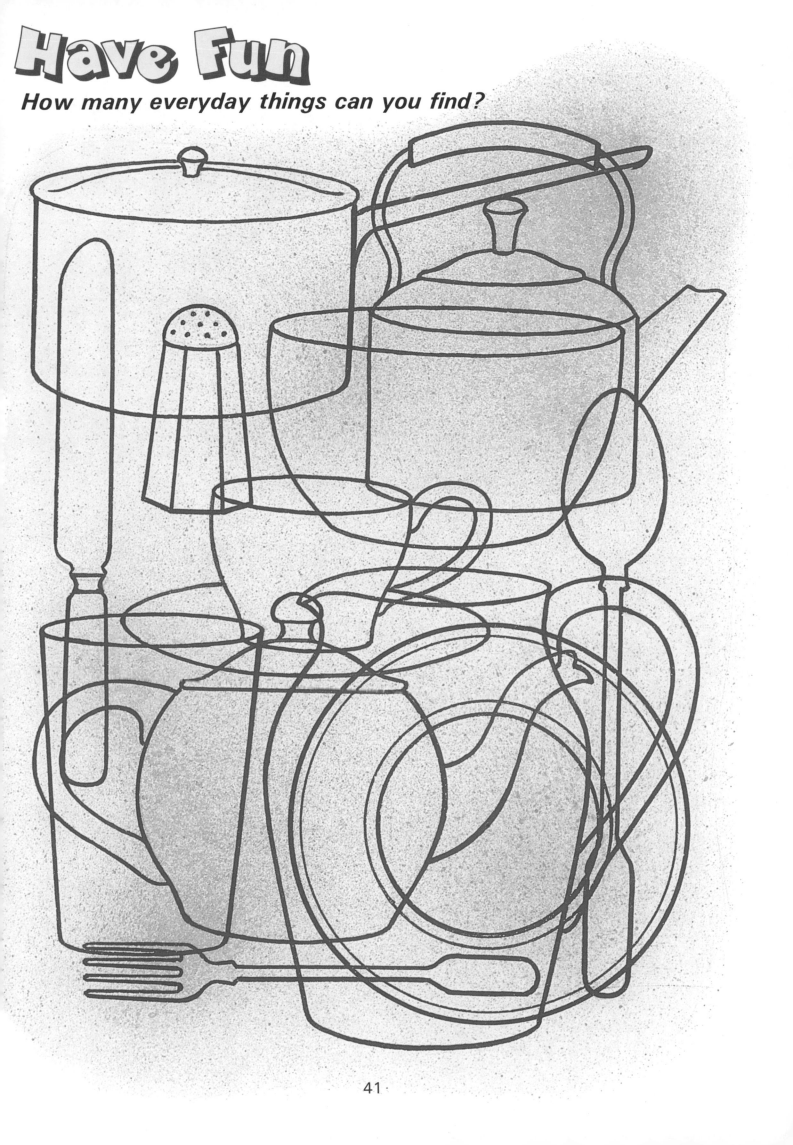

Mary had a little lamb
Its fleece was black as soot,
and into Mary's bread and jam
His sooty foot he put.

Have Fun

**Which way must Robin Hood take to escape
from the Sheriff and his men?**

There was an old man from Whitehaven
Whose beard had never been shaven.
    He said, 'It is best,
    For it makes a nice nest
In which I can keep my pet raven.'

'Knock, knock!'
'Who's there?'
'Justin.'
'Justin who?'
'Justin time
for a cup of tea!'

'Oh dear, I've lost my dog!'
'Why not advertise for him
in the paper?'
'It's no good. He can't read.'

'Nellie, have you changed
the water in the goldfish bowl?'
'No, it hasn't drunk
the last lot yet.'

'Potterton, what does
"out of bounds" mean?'
'A tired kangaroo.'

What should you do
if you split your sides
laughing?
*Run until you get
a stitch in them!*

'I know a boy
who can imitate birds.'
'Does he whistle?'
'No. He eats worms.'

Why do witches fly on broomsticks?
*If they flew on vacuum cleaners
the cords wouldn't be long enough!*

'Willie, if you had five pounds in one pocket
and two pounds in the other,
what would you have?'
'Someone else's trousers!'

Have Fun

*Whose horse? Trace the tangled reins to find which horse
belongs to which cowboy.*

'You're much too fat.
You must get more exercise.
Take up golf!'

'It's no good, Doctor.
If I put the ball where I can hit it,
I can't see it.

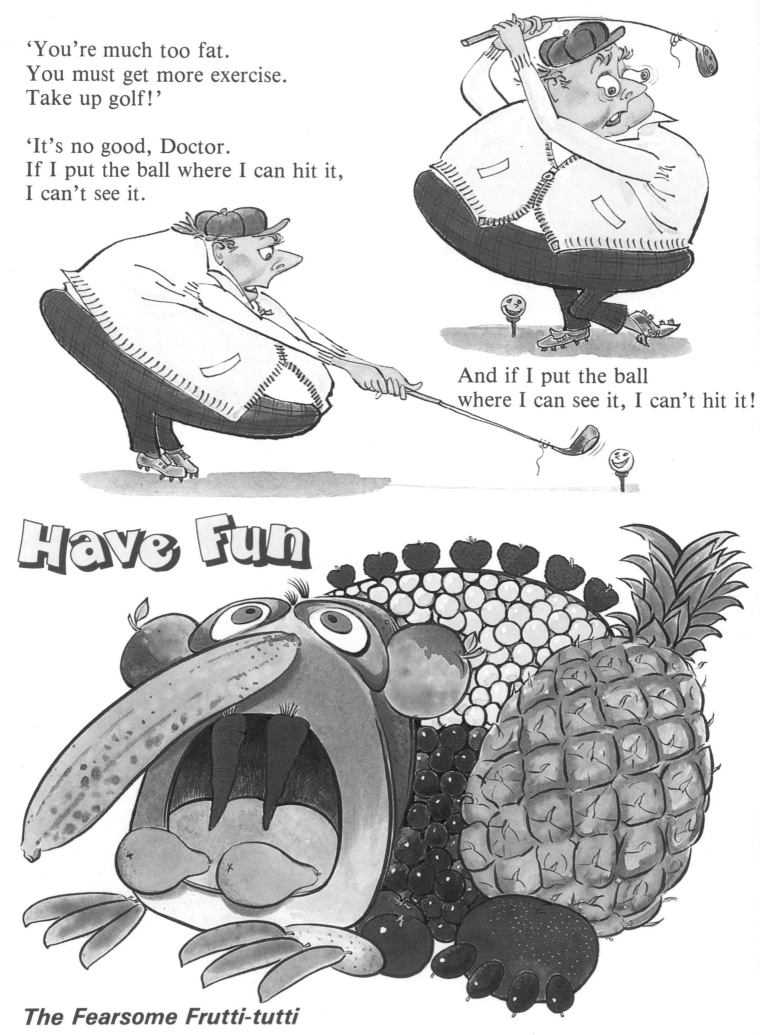

And if I put the ball
where I can see it, I can't hit it!

Have Fun

The Fearsome Frutti-tutti

From which fruits and vegetables has the Frutti-tutti been made?

'Knock, knock!'
'Who's there?'
'Robin.'
'Robin who?'
'Robin and stealing
will get you in jail!'

'Have you heard the story
about the dirty window?'

'No, what is it?'

'You wouldn't see
through it!'

A llama that came from Peru
Once spat at a girl in the zoo.
   Said the keeper, 'Now llama,
   You mustn't alarm 'er —
You'd not like her to do it to you!'

'Mum, they're not growing
bananas any longer.'
'Aren't they, Willie? Why not?'
'They're long enough already!'

'You look badly knocked about. Have you had an accident?'

'It wasn't an accident. I was tossed by a bull and he did it on purpose!'

'Why does your dog turn round and round before he lies down, Nellie?'
'Because he's a watch dog. He has to wind himself up!'

'Knock, knock!'
'Who's there?'
'Willie.'
'Willie who?'
'Willie lend me his bike?'

What is the biggest moth?
A mammoth!

'Jimmy, there's no such word as "can't".'
'Have you ever tried striking a match on butter, Miss?'

This word looks like what it means

Now, on a separate piece of paper, make these words look like what they mean –
CLOUDS   WOBBLY   EXPLOSION

There is a young lady whose nose
Continually prospers and grows;
  When it grew out of sight
  She exclaimed in a fright,
'Oh! Farewell to the end of my nose!'

Edward Lear

Which animal can you never trust?.....*A cheetah!*

Nervous air-passenger
Captain, you will bring us down safely, won't you?
Pilot
Don't worry, madam.
I've never left anyone up there yet!

Have Fun

Find the cat's name hidden in her picture!

Five French friars fanning funny fleas.

What does a flea do
when it gets angry?
It gets hopping mad!

'Doctor, doctor! I've swallowed a spoon!'
'Sit down and don't stir!'

If a Red Indian's wife is a squaw,
what is a Red Indian's baby?
A squawker!

In Africa, where coconuts grow,
A beetle stepped on an elephant's toe.
The elephant said, with tearful eyes,
'Pick on a feller of your own size!'

'I saw six ladies under one umbrella
and no one got wet.'
'It must have been a big umbrella,
Nellie.'
'No – it wasn't raining!'

His mother cried, 'Now Egbert, stop!
You really mustn't drink more pop.'
But Egbert loved its bubbly feeling.
He drank — and popped up to the ceiling.

P.Y.

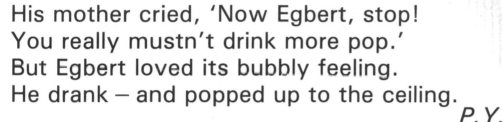

Have Fun

Make your own picture
of an Amazing Animal
like the Frutti-tutti
or the Snapping Snort-hopper.
If you wish, you can paste it on a card,
draw wavy lines down and across it
and cut it up into a jig-saw.
That would really
be a puzzle for your friends!

'Knock, knock!'
'Who's there?'
'Mike.'
'Mike who?'
'My cat's had kittens!'

'What do you get if you cross a cow
with a duck, Potterton?'
'Cream quackers, naturally.'

Tabby Cat Did you go in
for the Milk Drinking Competition?
Ginger Tom Yes — I won by ten laps.

You said you would take
Willie to the zoo today.

If the zoo wants Willie,
they can come and get him!

Have Fun

Amaze your friends
by playing the Paper-and-Comb!
Fold a piece of tissue
or grease-proof paper over a comb.
Hold it very gently to your lips
and hum into it.
You should hum through your lips
so that you feel the paper tickling your lips.
That's the secret!
Experiment until you get the sound coming out
through your Paper-and-Comb.

Now, with your shaker,
you are on the way to being a One-Man Band!

'Doctor, how did you know
I needed glasses?'
'Oh, I could tell as soon
as you walked through the window.'

'Is there any *kind of cake you don't like, Potterton?'*
'Yes, stomach-ache.'

DOWN
IN
THE
MOUTH
by MONA LOTT

How do you keep cool
at a football match?
Stand by a fan!

What's yellow and has greasy wings?
A bread and butterfly!

ABRACADABRA!
What vanished?
Find all that is hidden
in the picture.

What goes 99 – plonk?
A centipede with a wooden leg!

What keys cannot turn locks?
Monkeys or donkeys!

Have Fun

How many fish are hiding from the fisherman?

What's green and jumps around the garden?
Spring cabbage!

How do you make a bandstand?
Take away the chairs!

Have Fun

Starting at the spot on the lid, can you find a way through the maze?

One of the tortoises is facing in the opposite direction to the others. Can you find which one?

What stays hot in a refrigerator?
Mustard!

What's yellow and stupid?
Thick custard!

How did Noah see in the dark?
He turned on the floodlights!

Doctor Bell fell down the well
And broke his collar-bone.
Doctors should attend the sick –
And leave the well alone!

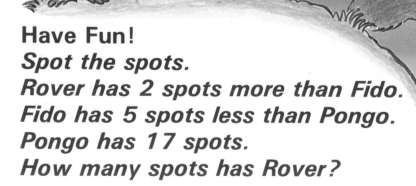

Have Fun!
Spot the spots.
Rover has 2 spots more than Fido.
Fido has 5 spots less than Pongo.
Pongo has 17 spots.
How many spots has Rover?

Have Fun

Have Fun

This word looks like what it means

CRACKED

Now, on a separate piece of paper, make these words look like what they mean –

GHOST   **LIGHTNING**   **WAVES**

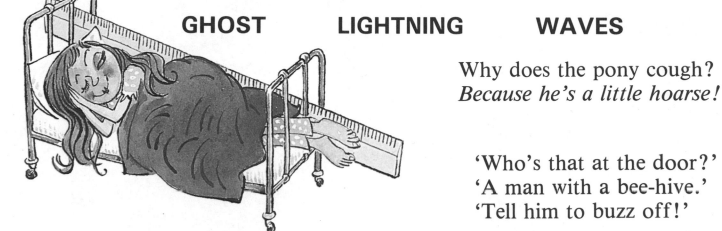

Why does the pony cough?
Because he's a little hoarse!

'Who's that at the door?'
'A man with a bee-hive.'
'Tell him to buzz off!'

Why should you take a ruler to bed with you?
To see how long you sleep!

Where do you find giant snails?
On giants' fingers!

The
SANDCASTLE
by C SHAW

Howler
The Equator is a menagerie lion running round the Earth.